piano ◆ vocal ◆ guitar

BOBBY Darin

songbook

T0083910

ISBN 1-4234-0408-4

HAL•LEONARD®
CORPORATION
7777 W. BLUEMOUND RD. P.O. BOX 13819 MILWAUKEE, WI 53213

For all works contained herein:
Unauthorized copying, arranging, adapting, recording or public performance is an infringement of copyright.
Infringers are liable under the law.

Visit Hal Leonard Online at
www.halleonard.com

contents

6 About a Quarter to Nine

10 Artificial Flowers

14 Beyond the Sea

22 Bill Bailey, Won't You Please Come Home

18 Call Me Irresponsible

25 Clementine

34 Dream Lover

38 Eighteen Yellow Roses

43 Hello, Dolly!

46 Hello, Young Lovers

52 If I Were a Carpenter

54 Lazy River

57 Lovin' You

62 Mack the Knife

66 **More (Ti Guarderò Nel Cuore)**

70 Multiplication

74 A Nightingale Sang in Berkeley Square

79 **Queen of the Hop**

84 Simple Song of Freedom

96 Splish Splash

88 **That's All**

92 Things

99 What'd I Say

104 **You Must Have Been a Beautiful Baby**

107 You're the Reason I'm Living

BIOGRAPHY

Darin! A member of that elite group of entertainers—Sinatra!... Ella!... Sammy!... Elvis!—who were recognizable by a single name and whose talent was so unique and innovating that they populate a separate category unto themselves.

Bobby Darin was born Walden Robert Cassotto on May 14, 1936 in the Bronx, New York City. Saddled with a delicate heart from birth, he contracted rheumatic fever at an early age and was not expected to live past his teens. But as he did his entire life, Darin defied the odds and through his relentless drive and self-taught show-biz savvy went on to become first, a teen idol, then a jazz-influenced pop singer, a movie and television star, and, ultimately, a live performer nonpareil.

Originally signed to Decca Records and dropped, he was about to be dropped by his second label, Atco, when he wrote and recorded a novelty song called "Splish Splash," which shot up to #3 on the charts in 1958. He followed that up with "Early in the Morning," "Queen of the Hop," "Plain Jane," and the enchanting "Dream Lover," all reaching the Top 40 within a 12-month period. Then in 1959, in a career-defining gamble, he abandoned his teen-idol status and recorded an album of big band standards that contained two of his most famous songs, "Mack the Knife" and "Beyond the Sea." "Mack the Knife" went on to hold the #1 position for nine weeks and stayed on the charts for six months. It also won Darin two GRAMMY Awards®—one for Record of the Year and the first GRAMMY® awarded for Best New Artist.

From there it was an easy jump to the big screen. He made his motion picture debut in *Come September*, where he met his first wife, Sandra Dee, the mother of his only child, Dodd Mitchell Darin. Dramatic turns followed with *Hell Is for Heroes*, *Pressure Point*, and *Captain Newman, M.D.*, for which he received an Academy Award nomination as Best Supporting Actor. During this period, he was also a ubiquitous presence on television and became the youngest performer to headline his own network special, *Bobby Darin and Friends*, on NBC in 1960.

He also continued to score Top 40 hits with "Clementine," "Bill Bailey, Won't You Please Come Home," "Artificial Flowers," "Lazy River," "Irresistible You," "Multiplication," "Things," and "You Must Have Been a Beautiful Baby." The composer of the latter, the renowned Johnny Mercer, once stated that he loved all the wonderful singers who performed his songs—which took in a lot of ground—but that, in his estimation, "Bobby was the best."

But perhaps Darin's most indelible talent was as a live performer. To witness a Bobby Darin show was to remain electrified well beyond the final curtain. He sang, played a half-dozen instruments, did comedy and impressions, and punctuated his performances with a unique set of moves that became his trademark. His only serious "in person" rival was the multi-talented Sammy Davis Jr., who could exhaust an audience with his explosive stage persona. Yet, when asked if there was anyone *he* would not attempt to follow, Davis said without hesitation, "Bobby Darin."

As an interpreter of songs, he "studied" under the masters. He idolized Al Jolson, Bing Crosby, Ray Charles, and Frank Sinatra. Accused of possessing an inordinate amount of cockiness, Darin was always good press. He was terribly misquoted after he won his two GRAMMYs® when a reporter wrote that the 23-year-old Darin said that he wanted to be bigger than Frank Sinatra. The press jumped on this and attempted to create a feud between the two. Some years later, Sinatra was asked about his feud with Darin. Ol' Blue Eyes said, "What feud? I'm his biggest fan. He's the heir apparent."

Highly committed to the civil rights movement, Bobby shifted musical gears once again as the 1960s wound down. He began exploring the intricacies of folk and protest music and scored a major hit in 1968 with a Tim Hardin composition, "If I Were a Carpenter." Returning the favor, Darin wrote Hardin's only charting record, "Simple Song of Freedom," a piece that has emerged as one of the finest protest statements of the era and one that Bobby himself performed at every show for the rest of his life.

In the early 1970s, while in production on his NBC variety series, *The Bobby Darin Show*, Darin's fragile health began to fail drastically. During a performance, he would drain his physical resources so completely that he would have to sneak off-stage to breathe from an ever-present oxygen tank. Yet audiences never knew the severity of his condition and were never the recipients of anything less than a bravura, no-holds-barred performance. Finally, on December 20, 1973, at the age of 37, Bobby Darin died while undergoing an operation in an attempt to repair his delicate heart.

Bobby Darin was a consummate performer. He is a legend whose accomplishments in every facet of the entertainment industry included those as a singer, actor, songwriter, nightclub performer, record producer, talent scout, music publisher, television star, and film scorer. And all this was accomplished in a ridiculously short 15-year career. He was elected to the Rock 'n' Roll Hall of Fame in 1999. He is as popular today as he was during his lifetime. A major motion picture based on his life, *Beyond the Sea*, directed by and starring Kevin Spacey, was released in 2004 and his musical legacy continues to bring to light his boundless talent.

We shall never see his like again.

—*James Ritz*

ABOUT A QUARTER TO NINE

Words by AL DUBIN
Music by HARRY WARREN

© 1935 WARNER BROS. INC. (Renewed)
All Rights Reserved   Used by Permission

ARTIFICIAL FLOWERS

Lyrics by SHELDON HARNICK
Music by JERRY BOCK

© 1960 (Renewed 1988) MAYERLING PRODUCTIONS, LTD. (Administered by R&H MUSIC) and JERRY BOCK ENTERPRISES
All Rights outside the United States Controlled by ALLEY MUSIC CORP. and TRIO MUSIC COMPANY
All Rights Reserved   Used by Permission

spair.

Additional Lyrics

2. Did you hear this poor little child was only nine years of age
   When mother and dad went away?
   Still she bravely worked at the one thing she knew,
   To earn a few pennies a day.

   (To Chorus 1)

3. With paper and shears, with wire and wax,
   She made up each tulip and mum.
   As snowflakes drifted in her tenement room,
   Her baby little fingers grew numb.

   Chorus:
   From artificial flowers, those artificial flowers,
   Flowers for ladies of high fashion to wear.
   She made artificial flowers, artificial flowers,
   Fashioned from Annie's despair.

4. They found little Annie all covered with ice
   Still clutching her poor frozen shears,
   Amidst all the blossoms she had fashioned by hand
   And watered with all her young tears.

5. There must be a heaven where little Annie can play
   In heavenly gardens and bowers,
   And instead of a halo, she'll wear 'round her head
   A garland of genuine flowers.

   Chorus:
   No more artificial flowers, artificial flowers,
   Flowers for ladies of society to wear.
   Those artificial flowers, artificial flowers,
   Fashioned from Annie's,
   (To Chorus 1Fashioned from Annie's despair.

BEYOND THE SEA

Words and Music by CHARLES TRENET,
ALBERT LASRY and JACK LAWRENCE

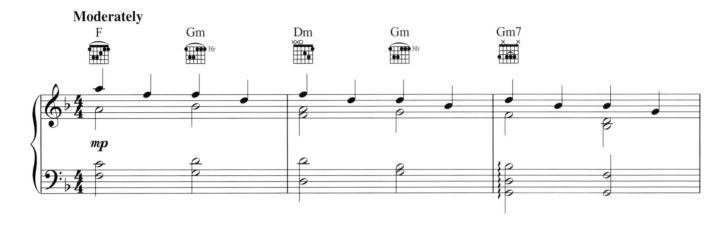

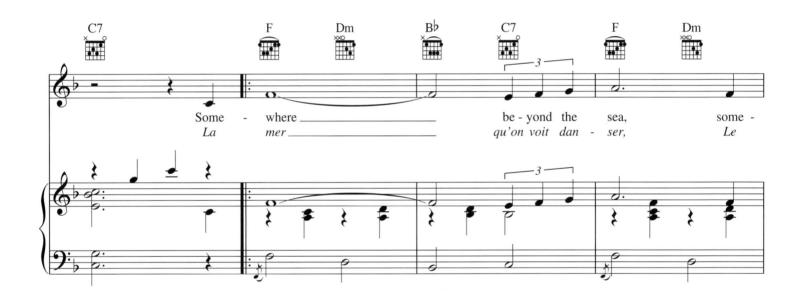

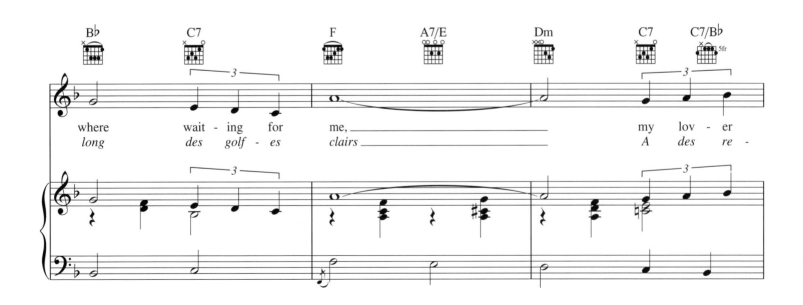

Copyright © 1945, 1946, 1947 (Renewed) by France Music Corp. and Range Road Music Inc.
All Rights Reserved   Used by Permission

CALL ME IRRESPONSIBLE
from the Paramount Picture PAPA'S DELICATE CONDITION

Words by SAMMY CAHN
Music by JAMES VAN HEUSEN

Copyright © 1962, 1963 (Renewed 1990, 1991) by Paramount Music Corporation
International Copyright Secured   All Rights Reserved

BILL BAILEY, WON'T YOU PLEASE COME HOME

Words and Music by
HUGHIE CANNON

Copyright © 1995 by HAL LEONARD CORPORATION
International Copyright Secured   All Rights Reserved

CLEMENTINE

Words and Music by
WOODY HARRIS

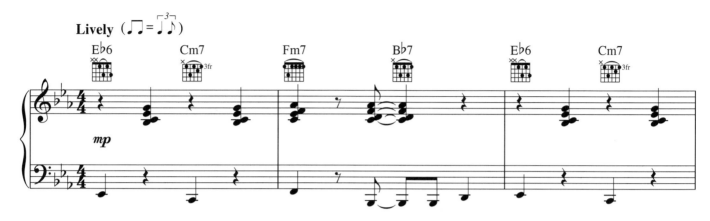

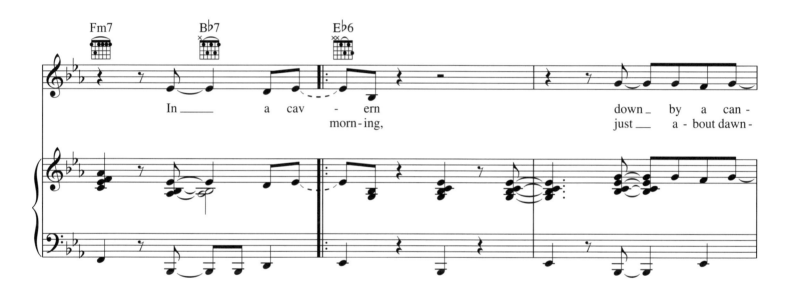

In ___ a cav - ern
morn - ing,

down ___ by a can -
just ___ a - bout dawn -

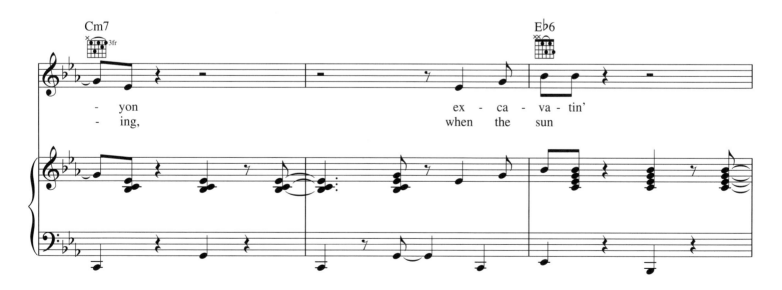

- yon
- ing,

ex - ca - va - tin'
when the sun

© 1960 (Renewed) Anna Teresa Music Ltd. and Ellipsis Music
All Rights Reserved

DREAM LOVER

Words and Music by
BOBBY DARIN

Copyright © 1959 by Alley Music Corp. and Trio Music Company
Copyright Renewed
International Copyright Secured   All Rights Reserved
Used by Permission

EIGHTEEN YELLOW ROSES

Words and Music by
BOBBY DARIN

Moderately

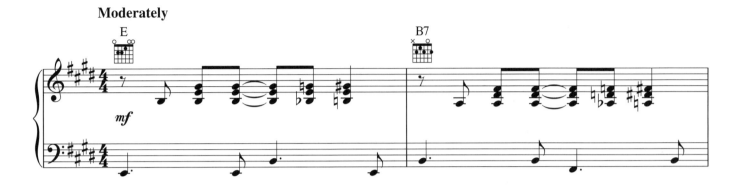

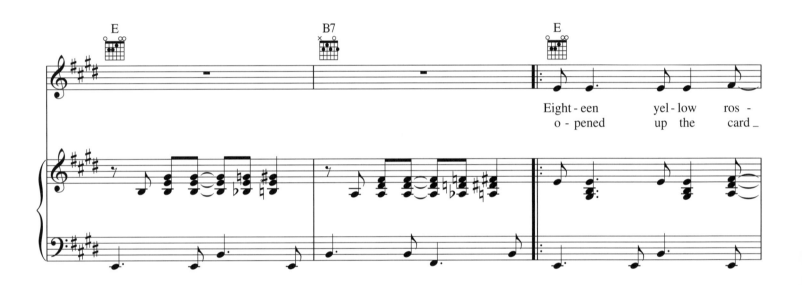

Eight- een   yel- low   ros -
o - pened   up the   card

- es   came   to - day, ___
___ to   see   what it   said. ___

Copyright © 1963 by Alley Music Corp. and Trio Music Company
Copyright Renewed
International Copyright Secured   All Rights Reserved
Used by Permission

day. _____ I nev-er doubt-

-ed your love ___ for a min-ute;

I al-ways thought that you ___ would be true.

But now, ___ this box ___ and the flow-ers

HELLO, DOLLY!

Music and Lyric by
JERRY HERMAN

© 1963 (Renewed) JERRY HERMAN
All Rights Controlled by EDWIN H. MORRIS & COMPANY, A Division of MPL Music Publishing, Inc.
All Rights Reserved

44

HELLO, YOUNG LOVERS
from THE KING AND I

Lyrics by OSCAR HAMMERSTEIN II
Music by RICHARD RODGERS

Copyright © 1951 by Richard Rodgers and Oscar Hammerstein II
Copyright Renewed
WILLIAMSON MUSIC owner of publication and allied rights throughout the world
International Copyright Secured   All Rights Reserved

IF I WERE A CARPENTER

Words and Music by
TIM HARDIN

Copyright © 1966 (Renewed) Allen Stanton Productions
International Copyright Secured   All Rights Reserved
Used by Permission

LAZY RIVER

Words and Music by HOAGY CARMICHAEL
and SIDNEY ARODIN

Copyright © 1931 by Peermusic Ltd.
Copyright Renewed
International Copyright Secured   All Rights Reserved

LOVIN' YOU

Words and Music by
JOHN SEBASTIAN

Copyright © 1966, 1967 by Alley Music Corp. and Trio Music Company
Copyright Renewed
International Copyright Secured   All Rights Reserved
Used by Permission

MACK THE KNIFE

English Words by MARC BLITZSTEIN
Original German Words by BERT BRECHT
Music by KURT WEILL

© 1928 UNIVERSAL EDITION
© 1955 WEILL-BRECHT-HARMS CO., INC.
Renewal Rights Assigned to the KURT WEILL FOUNDATION FOR MUSIC, BERT BRECHT and Edward and Josephine Davis, as Executors of the ESTATE OF MARC BLITZSTEIN
All Rights Reserved   Used by Permission

MORE
(Ti Guarderò Nel Cuore)

Music by NINO OLIVIERO and RIZ ORTOLANI
Italian Lyrics by MARCELLO CIORCIOLINI
English Lyrics by NORMAN NEWELL

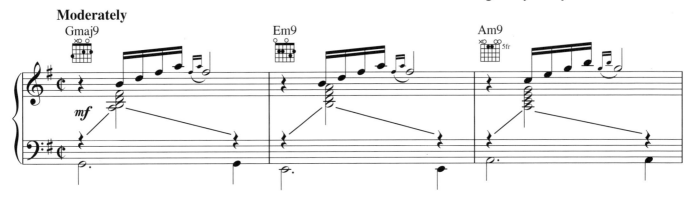

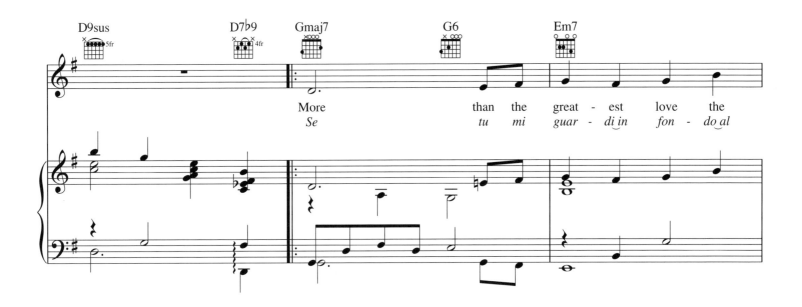

More than the great-est love the
Se tu mi guar-di in fon-do al

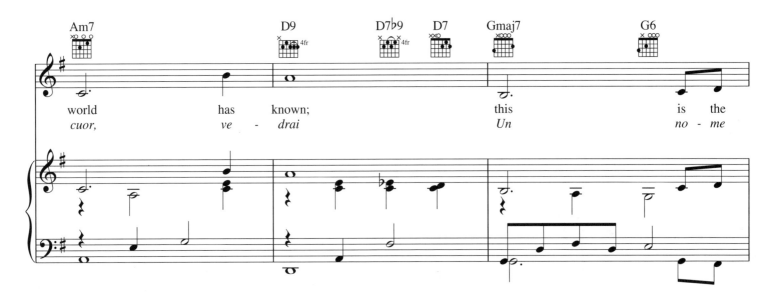

world has known; this is the
cuor, ve-drai Un no-me

Copyright © 1962 by C.A.M. S.r.l. - Rome (Italy), Via Cola di Rienzo, 152
International Copyright Secured   All Rights Reserved

MULTIPLICATION

Words and Music by
BOBBY DARIN

Copyright © 1961 by Alley Music Corp. and Trio Music Company
Copyright Renewed
International Copyright Secured   All Rights Reserved
Used by Permission

A NIGHTINGALE SANG IN BERKELEY SQUARE

Lyric by ERIC MASCHWITZ
Music by MANNING SHERWIN

When true lov-ers meet in May-fair, so the leg-ends tell, song birds sing, win-ter turns to spring, ev-'ry wind-ing street in May-fair falls be-neath the spell. I

Copyright © 1940 The Peter Maurice Music Co., Ltd., London, England
Copyright Renewed and Assigned to Shapiro, Bernstein & Co., Inc., New York for U.S.A. and Canada
International Copyright Secured   All Rights Reserved
Used by Permission

*Pronounced "Bar-kley"

QUEEN OF THE HOP

Words and Music by WOODY HARRIS
and BOBBY DARIN

Copyright © 1958 Walden Music Corp. and Tweed Music Co.
Copyright Renewed, Assigned to Anna Teresa Music Ltd. and Ellipsis Music Corp.
All Rights Reserved
Reprinted by Permission

D.S. al Coda

Oh, well, she

CODA

does the stroll. Oh, well, I love my queen. Do you

know who I mean? Sweet lit-tle six - teen;

SIMPLE SONG OF FREEDOM

Words and Music by
BOBBY DARIN

Come and sing a sim - ple song of free - dom.

- dom. _____ Sing it like _____ you've

nev - er sung be - fore. _____

Copyright © 1969 by Alley Music Corp. and Trio Music Company
Copyright Renewed
International Copyright Secured   All Rights Reserved
Used by Permission

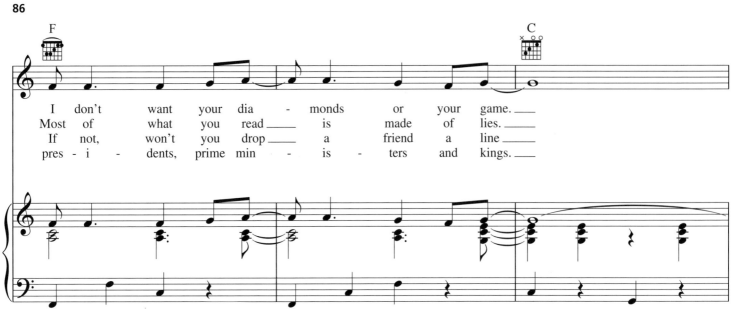

THAT'S ALL

Words and Music by BOB HAYMES
and ALAN E. BRANDT

© 1953 (Renewed) WARNER-TAMERLANE PUBLISHING CORP. and MIXED BAG MUSIC INC.
All Rights Administered by WARNER-TAMERLANE PUBLISHING CORP.
All Rights Reserved   Used by Permission

THINGS

Words and Music by
BOBBY DARIN

Copyright © 1961, 1962 by Alley Music Corp. and Trio Music Company
Copyright Renewed
International Copyright Secured   All Rights Reserved
Used by Permission

SPLISH SPLASH

Words and Music by BOBBY DARIN
and MURRAY KAUFMAN

Copyright © 1958 by Unart Music Corporation
Copyright Renewed and Assigned to Alley Music Corp., Trio Music Company and Unart Music Corporation
All Rights on behalf of Unart Music Corporation Assigned to EMI Catalogue Partnership and Controlled and Administered by EMI Unart Catalog Inc.
International Copyright Secured   All Rights Reserved
Used by Permission

WHAT'D I SAY

Words and Music by
RAY CHARLES

Copyright © 1959 by Unichappell Music Inc.
Copyright Renewed
International Copyright Secured   All Rights Reserved

YOU MUST HAVE BEEN A BEAUTIFUL BABY

Words by JOHNNY MERCER
Music by HARRY WARREN

© 1938 WARNER BROS. INC. (Renewed)
All Rights Reserved Used by Permission

YOU'RE THE REASON I'M LIVING

Words and Music by
BOBBY DARIN

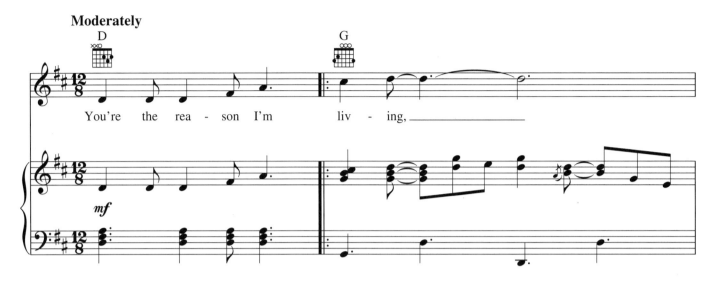

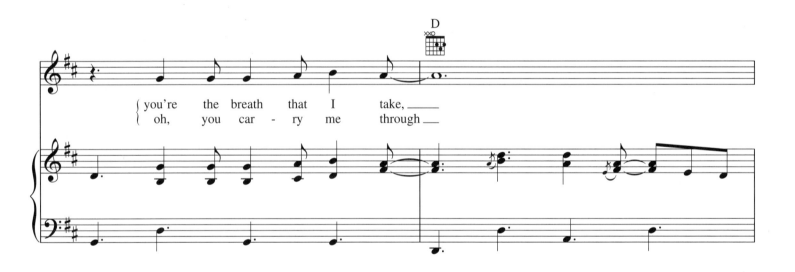

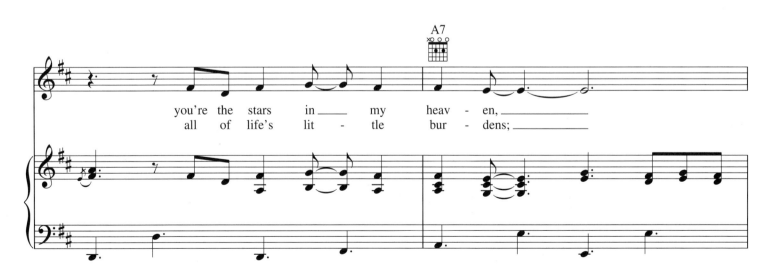

Copyright © 1962, 1963 by Alley Music Corp. and Trio Music Company
Copyright Renewed
International Copyright Secured All Rights Reserved
Used by Permission